Resilient Heart:

The Healing Power of Art

Katelyn Mariah

BFA, MA, LICSW (Emirates) 2018

MYSTICK CREEK
PUBLISHING

1641 Hague Ave, St. Paul, MN 55104

651-955-3673

Resilient Heart Art

Copyright 2018 by Katelyn Mariah

All rights reserved, Published by Mystick Creek Publishing. No part of this book or artwork may be reproduced or transmitted in any form or by any means, electronic or mechanical, including photocopying, recording, or by any information storage and retrieval system, without the written permission from the publisher. For information address Mystick Creek Publishing 1641 Hague Ave, St. Paul, MN 55104 www.mystickcreekpublishing.com   mystickcreekpublishing@gmail.com

ISBN-13: 978-0-9970215-3-0

First Edition, August 2018

Printed in the United States of America

TABLE OF CONTENTS
CHAPTER ONE: INTRODUCTION...page 4
CHAPTER TWO: ABOUT KATELYN'S ART...page 6
CHAPTER THREE: REFLECTIONS ON KATELYN'S ART...page 8
CHAPTER FOUR: HEALING POWER OF ART...page 11
CHAPTER FIVE: HEART HEALING IMAGES/DIALOGUES...page 17
CHAPTER SIX: ABOUT KATELYN...page 85

CHAPTER ONE
INTRODUCTION

This book is the companion to Resilient Heart: A Holistic Approach to a Healthy Heart for Women, where you can read about my personal journey and everything I learned about heart health. As a trained art-therapist I know the power of art to heal and use it as a tool my when going through a healing process. As a visionary artist my art takes me to places within me that I would never discover on my own and brings them to light in images. The paintings in this book follow my healing journey as I recovered from three heart attacks over a period of ten months and open-heart surgery, all of which happening in two years. These paintings were a big part of my healing process.

Why Paint a series of paintings?

When I had the 2nd heart attack in Austria I got the message during meditation that I needed to do a series of paintings of aspects of the heart and they would help me heal. I had already done four paintings at that point, so it made sense to continue. I have done series of paintings before and I understood that the process was you paint until it ends naturally. This series continued for over a year and I ended up painting 32 paintings.

From August 10-2017 to May 10, 2018 I did 27 paintings. The closer I got to healing the faster they came. From January 2018 to May of 2018 I painted 15 painting. As you follow the images and the information and guidance I received with each painting you will understand how it supported my healing process.

One thing you should know before entering this journey is I don't have preconceived ideas going into a painting. I have a blank slate where inspiration comes to me and I paint it. So, each of these images came to me from another realm. I don't think about symbolism or meaning at all. My soul speaks, and I listen. I do research after I paint to see if there are connections I should be aware of. There always are!

Another thing that is important to know is where my art comes from. One Winter, years ago, I was not in a good place about my life. I remember looking out the window at the trees which all looked dead and thinking " They look dead but there is so much life happening underneath the ground that we don't see." I decided that I would paint what we don't see, underneath, around, above, below. You will often see panels in my paintings. There is always a main image and the panels show us what we don't see. A slice of the hidden world. I still paint this way today.

Join me as we follow my muse on this heart healing journey...

CHAPTER TWO
ABOUT KATELYN'S VISIONARY ART PROCESS

My philosophy about Visionary Art

To the visionary artist every work of art embodies their inner vision and at the same time reveals a facet of the collective mind. My images arise from an innate personal vision that reveals itself to me through the creative process as I follow my inner promptings.

I attempt to make my inner world and the collective consciousness visible to myself and the viewer. I paint what others don't see and the image becomes a doorway into that realm, which the viewer can enter. Thus, my visionary work creates images that activate inner wisdom in the viewer. Here an energetic dialog occurs that touches the psyche through an interchange of color, symbol, metaphor, movement, and space, so the painting speaks the language of the soul. The images invite the viewer to move to a place within which connects them to their well of higher wisdom to find insight.

Being an artist is a sacred responsibility and in doing my job well, my work will speak to our collective experience, so we feel less separate and more whole.

My art has always been about personal development and self-discovery. In my mid 30's it became visionary as well. When I tap into the visionary part of me I am looking for a way to bring the unknown to light. This life affirming imagery is what I share through my paintings.

I use the Mischtechnik because it lends itself to the spiritual nature of the art work. I also work in watercolor. The Mischtecknik creates the image out of high light rather than shadow, focusing the process to build the image out of layering a series of chromatic glazes that build from primary colors to local color. Through this process there is more depth, luminosity, etheric qualities and unusual color in the painting. Mischtechnik paintings, when done well glow with inner light.

I create images that are fresh and engaging yet deeply powerful. Images that make you pause and wonder. Some of the most powerful images are ones that don't have a logical meaning and force you to bypass thinking. These images plant seeds that nudge the viewer's consciousness to move to a new level.

The artist serves to remind us of the sacredness of life by creating a picture of our transformative and spiritual potential. Visionary art is an alchemical journey that brings together of spirit and matter into a united whole It is the task of the visionary artist to take the pilgrimage to the inner landscape, connect with the wisdom that dwells there and bring it forward for other, through the image.

Art awakens subtle emotions, of a spiritual nature that are powerful yet nameless. The artist who lets the creative process move through her/him, can experience being lifted out of a chaotic feeling state into a place of higher understanding by the very process of creating the image. The image and its resultant essential spirit has the ability to impact the in the same way and they discover insight and well-being. The meaning of the image becomes less important than the wisdom that is gained in the individual.

"It is my desire that my Art Work acts as a bridge between the physical reality and the metaphysical reality of metaphor and symbol that is the source of healing, transformation, beauty and Divine Love. I dedicate my work to creating products and services that support this vision to bring transformation and healing to others."
Kandinsky

CHAPTER THREE
REFLECTIONS ON KATELYN MARIAH'S ART

Reflections on Katelyn's art work given in 1996 by the late Ron Mangravite

Ron Mangravite was a Spiritual teacher who had a mystery school and an expert in the universal nature of symbolism, mysticism and mythology. He passed away in 1998. He spoke at the opening exhibition of her "Awaken The Goddess" meditation images. I met Ron at a monthly salon that my friend Dr. Jan Adams had each month. I had brought my Goddess paintings with me. We were sitting beside each other and I was showing him my work. I really had no idea who Ron was at the time, but he would become an important person in my life. He started talking about what he saw in my paintings and I was shocked. He in turn was surprised that I didn't know what I had painted. Here is his opening speech when we introduced Awakening the Goddess to the world:

"What I am here to share with you is some relatively academic knowledge which I thought was rather superficial and well known to Katelyn, but to my surprise, none of her work came out of academic studies. It just came up out of where it is supposed to come out of, which doesn't really happen much anymore. For me this presentation is a question of introducing a real live person who is doing extraordinary stuff.

This is not an opening of just some pretty exciting art, this is a public introduction to a woman who has found her inner identity in such a way that it transcends anything she is as a citizen, and inhabitant of Minneapolis, even as a woman and certainly as an artist.

I began studying exactly what is happening in the consciousness of a person who can get theses phenomenal telepathic test scores, who can heal someone by touching them with their hand, who can walk into a so called haunted house and precede to describe with relative accuracy the past history of some of the people who lived there. Where does that come from? Rather than saying that it's a weird thing, I wanted to know the why of it. The pursuit of that converts the searcher. I became a mystic and then discovered some of the things that are going to give me great pleasure to point out how Katelyn is also discovering these things.

If people have discovered that they are driven to this search to find mystical openings for some kind of spiritual awareness, they traditionally tried to find ways and means of allowing their inner cravings to somehow take form. They try to find ways to get them up and out of themselves and find a medium of expression. What people do if they are fortunate is to find an established group or teaching methods.

It was known that in order for a person to understand something of what lay ahead in the metaphysical path to enlightenment they had to first understand themselves. They had to understand and sort through their own identify and distinguish between those elements which were imposed by culture, and those elements which were genuine to them and those elements which were universal. this involved a tremendous amount of inner pain and searching because when you are trying to tell the difference between what is you and what is simply an appendage, the only way you can do it is to cut it and see if it bleeds. Artists who are working, whether in fiction, or the graphic arts, or in dance or anything else, know that if they are going to do something that has never been done before it has to be covered with their own blood. It has to be a thing that comes from a piece of their own flesh, taken out of the body and molded.

A master of such initiates would look at the images they dredge up from their subconscious and know instantly whether they were simply copying stuff that was in the air, whether they were taking designs from the wall, or whether they had found someone else's pictures. They would know whether this was their truth or not. If it was their truth this would have in fact been a masterpiece that would allow you to graduate and say, "I know my own identify, I am free to do this".

In attempting to find her identity, which is the Goddess, and find ways she could manifest, she apparently went down deep enough to get totally past Katelyn, to get totally past everything but her femininity, because these images are the Goddess. Katelyn dug down deep enough to get past anything that is the person and found real legitimate expressions that came from such a mixed bag of a culture that it would be very difficult for her to have truly cheated. She does not know that some of these symbols are Babylonian, Sumerian, Chinese, and Welsh. She could not possibly have known without at least 10 or 15 years of study. She could not have made this mixed bag up by faking it. It has to come from someplace very real.

And therefore, I am extremely privileged to be here to be more or less, the official midwife to announce to the world that this is not just an artist - Katelyn is an initiate of consciousness."

Ron Mangravite

CHAPTER FOUR

THE POWER OF ART TO HEAL

When the artist is alive in any person, whatever his kind of work may be, he becomes an inventive, searching, daring, self-expressing, creature. He becomes interesting to other people. He disturbs, upsets, enlightens and he opens the way for a better understanding.

Robert Henri

My heart loves to paint! It brings me joy. Maybe that is true for you as well or maybe you remember how it felt as a kid to have crayons and paper and just draw. I loved the box of 64 colors with the crayon sharpener build it!! The colors spoke to me.

The most important thing to remember when using art to heal is to have fun doing it. Your heart wants to have fun and it wants to express itself. Stay out of your head and let your heart speak through you. It is more about the process as you bring unconscious information into image that you were not in touch with before, than it is about a completed work of art. Everyone is an artist. We are all co-creating our lives each and every day and that is a very creative process! Creative expression is essential to well-being and the lack of it is causing disease. For most people the creative process stops at about 10 years old when someone laughs at something we painted, or the teacher tells us we can do a better job. Every time an attempt is made to draw something from that point on, we hear that laughter or the teacher's voice and we are a 10-year old that can't draw again. How many times have you heard someone say, "I can only draw stick people" That is because it is only stick people who can squeeze through the crack in the door that is closed to creativity.

People in the flow of creative energy are open, flexible, spontaneous and fearless. They are willing to take risks, make mistakes and have fun in the process because it is in the risk and mistake making that our greatest teachers live. In this flow of energy, the whole world opens up and blesses you. When you are in creative space you are connected to your Source, which is Love. Love is the energy of well-being and the place where healing happens.

I have been a visionary artist and writer for many years. After years of practice I have learned to get out of my own way when I am creating and open to inspiration. I wish I could do the same during the creation of everyday life. The word inspire comes from the Latin word 'inspirare' which means 'to breath into' or 'in'-into 'spirare' to breathe. Inspiration comes to us on the wings of the very breath we breathe. It can be just that easy if we are open and listening. Couple inspiration with imagination and you have manifestation. You get inspired, you imagine and have faith in a new future and it comes into manifestation.

We have learned about the importance of breathing consciously now see how it is connected to creativity. The simple act of conscious breathing, deeply into the diaphragm, can be a meditation in itself and it can have a profound impact on the ability to creatively open up. Taoist master Mantak Chia describes the diaphragm as nothing less than a spiritual muscle. He says; "Lifting the heart and fanning the fires of digestion and metabolism, the diaphragm muscle plays a largely unheralded role in maintaining our health, vitality, and well-being."

How do we bring the artist alive as Robert Henri suggests in the above quotation? I believe that we can make sacred the space in our inner and outer environment, so we can open up to the creative spirit. Creativity is born from the calm inner place that resides in the heart, not in the mind. It is the ability to invent, experiment, take risks, break rules, make mistakes and have fun doing it. We all have this ability and it is the stresses of life that make it difficult to access. From this space of innocence, imagination and play the door opens to our Inner Physician who is the voice of our body.

We each have our own unique form of creative expression. All we need to do to access this part of ourselves is step out of the way. For me mediation, music, journaling, movement and dance help me do that and open gateways to accessing my inner wise guide. I hope this inspires you to do the same.

We have lost touch with the ancient form of creating intentional art and it is through our reviving this tradition and seeing our creativity as a sacred act that we will be able to tap into this source of vast information that will guide our evolution. Begin today by being more mindful in your creative process and creating sacred space for the magic and mystery to dance. Everything exists in our imagination including perfect health and the process of making intentional art will set it free. Tap into your imagination and the Inner Physician and you will be amazed at what emerges to help you become well.

My post baccalaureate degree is in art therapy and I know that art and wellness go hand in hand. I have used art with clients but for the most part art therapy has been my path to growth and transformation. As a visionary artist and trained art therapist I consider art making a key part of my spiritual path. I am very interested in the relationship between art and spirituality and how art making can be a path that assists the artist in conscious evolution. Art reflects Spirit, both human and more-than-human.

Visual expression has been used for restoring health throughout history, but art therapy did not emerge as a distinct profession until the 1940s when artists working in psychiatric hospitals became aware that painting, drawing and other forms of artwork created the foundation for a therapeutic relationship between patient and therapist. The images that emerge from the unconscious reveal what is hidden and help the therapist gain a better understanding of the patient. It is the unconscious feelings and emotions that are creating disease and discomfort, so bringing them to light shifts perception. When I create a visionary image, it is brought up from deep within me and often I see things that I would have never seen through another means that end up transforming me.

Art is an important medium for communication because it is less threatening for the client than talking directly about a problem. Art therapy interventions can be specifically designed to address problems, so the client can integrate physical problems and emotional concerns, which is helpful because physical illness has an emotional component. In the same way, art can communicate with the artist and give them information about things they cannot see, such as illness and disease in the body. I have often finished a painting and upon observation discovered something about myself that had been hidden before the painting. This is one of the ways our Inner Physician communicates with us. Art therapy is a means for the patient to reconcile emotional conflicts, foster self-awareness, and express unspoken and frequently unconscious concerns about their disease and begin to have a dialog about them.

Carl Jung was known for his work with the mandala as well as visionary paintings in his own healing process and in working with clients. The mandala, which means 'circle' in Sanskrit, is a symbolic representation of the path to the center. The process of returning to center brings the body into balance. Creating mandalas can make the journey more meaningful and manageable, especially in the face of disease. Bonnie Bell, creator of the Gaia Star Mandalas said; "By gazing at a mandala, or by creating one ourselves, we tap into otherwise inaccessible sources of transformational help.

Whether we understand these sources to be within ourselves or coming from spirit beyond, we can be greatly enlivened by their gifts. . ... I speak of this art with passion because I have been helped very deeply by contemplating and creating mandalas. During a recent health crisis that could not really be addressed by allopathic medicine, these images have been a constant source of comfort and inspiration. In a very real way, I have drawn on mandalas as a source of 'beauty-medicine."

Mandalas are a form of intentional art, which is an object created with a specific intention. By infusing the artwork with intention, we strengthen the focus that we are working on. As the artist, we set a focus before creating the piece and infuse it with the spirit of the intention through the art making process. Art that is made with intention becomes medicine for the spirit and nourishment for the soul. For example, I made both a healing doll and a medicine pouch to take on a pilgrimage to Mexico and they have become powerful healing tools for me.

Art can be created to strengthen the energy around any intention, for example, creating prosperity, healing a specific illness, manifestation, or bringing a partner into your life. If the artist can create space that is sacred and step out of their own way, spirit will speak through them into the piece they are creating. The intention is strengthened by using it in ritual, by placing in on an altar or using it in meditation. Each piece has a spirit and radiance which speaks to the soul and can be used for personal healing or in healing work with other people. The Universe hears the request and comes to support that desire to heal on the physical plan. This act also engages the Inner Physician. I have made intentional art for myself as well as for others who have needed images of healing.

When I am in creative space, mystery unfolds before my eyes, and if I am able to step out of my way I create images that reflect something bigger, such as the images of the Goddess I painted. The process of creating art has taught me to relinquish my need to control and understand, so that I can connect with mystery and listen to its wisdom. Each piece of intentional art is created through an intuitive connection. If I am working with a client I connect with the client's inner being and wise one. I gather the information and create an object specific to the healing needs of the client, through dolls, soul portraits, shamanic rattles, medicine bags and portable shrines.

Visionary art making, whether it is writing, visual art, dance or music, is a shamanic process. Many artists have enhanced powers of seeing, hearing and dreaming, which allow them to move easily between the worlds, without experiencing the boundaries that keep others from exploring those realms. The artist often takes this journey for self-exploration but the images, movement, songs and poems that result, are transformational, enlightening, healing and empowering to those who experience their work.

I suggest you play around with different mediums to find the one that feels the best to you. I say play because I want you to be like the child when you explore the mediums and not get through off by fear of doing it right. That just gets in the way. Create a playground on which you begin to explore who you are through art and watch what happens.

The 32 images in this book were powerfully healing for me and I believe as you look at them and read my thoughts about them you will see why. As you explore them realize the images came first without any explanation and the works came from my guides and my research. Let the images speak to you, they might have something else to say to you.

Just dive in and let your creative child move through you. If you can do that you will be surprised at not only what you create but what it says to you. As you can see in my images I am following a theme which is the heart. Some images piggy back on each other and together they create a whole. If that starts to happen for you just follow it because it has an important story to tell you about healing yourself. You don't have to even understand what it is, just know that it is talking to you and your soul and you will get the message on some level.

CHAPTER FIVE
HEART HEALING IMAGES AND DIALOGUES

How this metaphysical heart journey began.

About 12 hours before I had the first heart attack, on the Spring Equinox of 2016, I had a dream. In the dream, other worldly beings put a star tetrahedron in my heart and a Vesica Pisces in my womb. I thought it had something to do with the Equinox. That was how this 24-month heart exploration and transformation began. This painting is the energetic depiction of that journey and where I am now.

I have been going through a huge change since the Solar Eclipse of March 8th, 2016. That particular eclipse occurred with the sun and moon at 18 degrees Pisces. When I looked at my natal chart my North Node was at 18 degrees Pisces. The North Node in your natal chart indicates what you are moving toward in life that is your destiny, the things you came to accomplish in this life time. I realized that this eclipse was telling me that I had a big opportunity to release what was keeping me from accomplishing my mission and I made a commitment to clear everything out.

I created a ritual to do that and wrote all of the things that I wanted to release on a piece of paper, which I took to my favorite place on the river and read out loud. It was a list of about 25 things some small and many of them big. After I was done I tore it up and placed in on a smoldering log that must have come from some party the night before. I made a list of all the things I wanted to welcome into my life and embrace and that was another very long list. With that list I waited until the exact moment when the eclipse would be half way through because in the vesica pisces the center is the most powerful part.

This is the Vesica Pisces

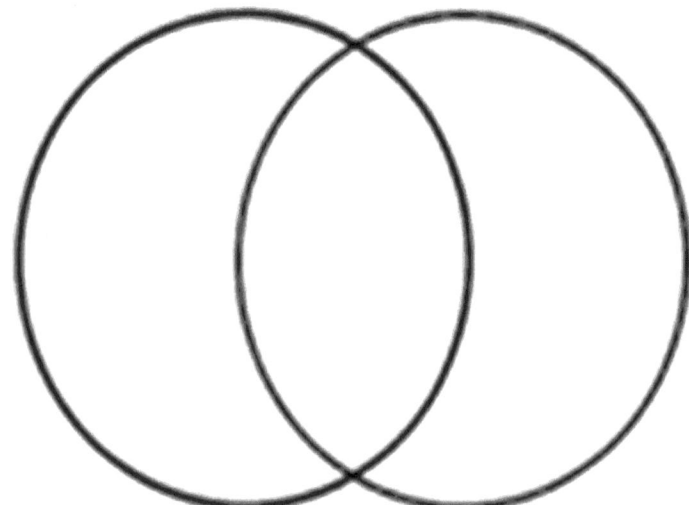

It is one of the oldest symbols on the planet and it represents the Mother God and Father God coming together to create offspring. The center of the symbol is where manifestation happens. I started researching and working with this symbol at the Solar Eclipse. There is a whole lot more about this symbol that I won't go into right now. The symbol for the Eclipse and the Equinox is the Vesica Pisces so it is about balancing masculine/feminine, dark and light.

After I did this ritual I was immediately sent into a transformational process that continued to the Spring Equinox, which was at 7:30 PM on March 19th. The Spring Equinox is when we have an equal amount of Dark and Light in a 24-hour period, so we are talking about balance again.

At 4 AM on March 20th I had a dream. A ritual was being performed for me and the Sacred Marriage, represented by the Six-Pointed Star and the Vesica Pisces were placed in my body. The Sacred Marriage was placed in my heart, and the Vesica Pisces in my Solar Plexus. The Solar Plexus is the vortex in our body where our personal power resides, so it made sense that the Vesica Pisces was placed there.

The Sacred Marriage/ Six-Pointed Star:

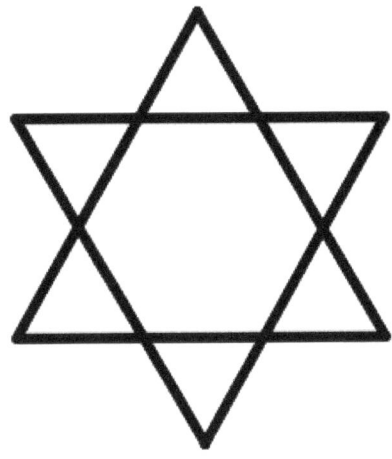

The Sacred Marriage is a two-fold process. It begins with the balance of the masculine and feminine within which leads to the ability to manifest a union in the outer world as a partnership with another. That cannot happen until your heart is open. I have been in this process for many years. Placing the Sacred Marriage in my heart activated that process internally in me at a whole other level. You will see these symbols in some of the paintings

Between 4 and 5 PM that night I had a heart attack....

Resilient Heart Art

Healing Heart Art #1

Painted: 3-26-2016

Title: The Pearls of my Heart

Symbolism: String of Pearls and Roses

This was painted after the first heart attack. I wanted a positive image I could focus on rather than focusing on how bad I felt. I had a Stress Induced Cardiomyopathy which is Broken Heart Syndrome. I didn't know I had a regular heart attack too. Broken Heart Syndrome made so much sense to me and I started to open to the idea that my heart was still broken and shielded from years ago. Now that it has broken open pearls and roses are coming out of it.

Pearls happen when a small object, such as sand, gets in the shell. As a defense to an irritant the mollusk creates a pearl to seal off the irritation. A substance called nacre or mother of pearl is deposited on the surface of the object, forming the pearl. The wound in the shell becomes the beautiful pearl just as our wounds can become beautiful if we let them. The painting suggested that a string of my heart-wounds had become beautiful pearls. I was creating a beautiful pearl metaphorically and it was running through the arteries of my heart.

Look at how nicely the rose fits into that metaphor. Since ancient times roses have been grown for their fragrance, beauty, and healing properties. Roses, with their unique combination of thorny stems and fragrant blossoms, are a symbol of achievement, completion and perfection: After having met the long stems with the thorns, you are rewarded with a flower of great beauty and mesmerizing fragrance. In other words, roses act as a metaphor for life and overcoming adversity.

Resilient Heart Art

Healing Heart Art #2

Painted: 4-1-2016

Title: The Genie in My Heart

My heart broke open, and the contents spilt out.

Like a genie in a bottle, waiting years to get back out.

Let the genie out of the bottle means allowing something to happen that cannot be stopped. Whatever was trapped in my heart that wanted to be released I wanted to let it out, so that my heart could open to love. Once you let the genie out of the bottle it is no longer possible to go back to a previous state. Those stored issues holding you back are released and the genie grants you 3 wishes. At this point in my healing I needed a genie to grant me three wishes to help me get healthy again.

So, who is the genie in the bottle/heart? Genies represent beings which exist in a realm that we can't see. The lamp is the connection between our world and a greater universe that we might not be aware of.

In the case of the magic lamp, the human body is the vessel (the lamp). The oil inside allows the lamp to be lit and to shine with light, comes from white light energy residing both within the body and in the aura. So, in the case of the painting is shows us that we have that light within our heart and we just need to allow it to shine.

By calling on the genie, we are calling on the genius that is inherent in each of us. We are the Genie. The Genie in the painting emerges from the heart lamp with all the tools she needs to navigate the world in a magical way.

Resilient Heart Art

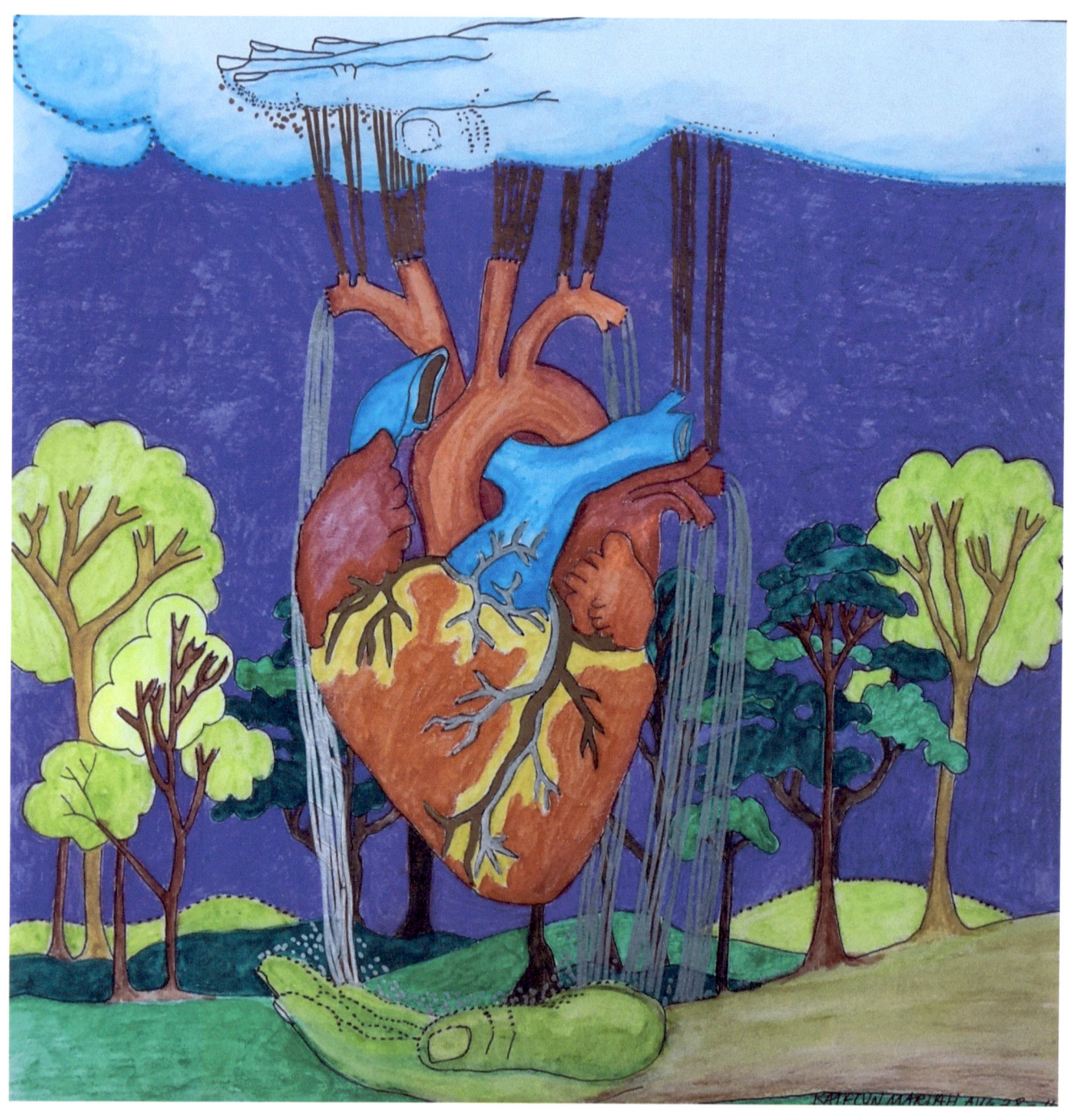

Healing Heart Art #3

Painted: 8-26-2016

Title: Mother Earth and Father Sky

This is how the forest helped me heal every time I went there. There is a healing force in nature that comes from the trees, from the sky and from the ground that supports healing in the body. This is my vision of it.

As you can see the hands of Father Sky are sending gold energy from above into the heart. Gold energy represents the masculine principle. Mother Earth is sending silver energy up from the ground into the heart. Silver energy represents the feminine principle.

I visited the forest hundreds of times during my heart recovery in all seasons. The trees helped me connected with the Divine Mother/Father energy, which in turn helped my heart heal. The heart in the painting is surrounded by the tree beings who are there to support the balancing and integration process.

As you also can see the arteries in the heart are silver and gold rather than red and blue, so the masculine and feminine energy is filling the heart and flowing into the body.

Resilient Heart Art

Healing Heart Art #4

Painted: 1-28-2017

Title: Triple Heart Transformation

When I painted this, I wanted to depict my emergence out of each heart attack. If you notice the bottom heart is less healthy then each of the hearts that follow until I emerge from the top heart which is healthy.

I thought it was the end of my heart journey and that my heart was healed. I am struck by the power and fierceness on the woman's face. That is how I felt at the time.

This was only 19 days after the third heart attack. I wanted to give myself an image of triumph that I could focus on moving forward.

I had been in a protective cocoon of peace and tranquility since I got out of the hospital. There was no thinking there. Just a sense of profound peace like I had never felt before. I am in receptive mode and that is when amazing art comes out of me.

From my journal around this time:

Imagine. Art that comes from a deep soul connection, that dances on paper, or canvas or in craft. This is art that is able to speak to you on a deep level and you understand because it speaks to your soul. You don't have to think about what you see. You can feel that it touches you, and you understand. That is visionary art and that is my gift. This is one of those paintings that speaks to your soul.

Resilient Heart Art

Healing Heart Art #5
Painted: 2-23-2017
Title: Yoga Heart

This image was another attempt at a book cover for Resilient Heart. I was looking for something that depicted peace and harmony, qualities we want to cultivate to keep our heart happy and healthy.

Yoga has a lot of benefits as far as the heart is concerned. Anyone who has had cardiac issues would find yoga helpful. If you would like to learn more there is a chapter dedicated to yoga in Resilient Heart: A holistic approach to a healthy heart for women.

Here is a woman with an open heart in the lotus pose. She has a heart at her throat and in her womb and she is holding a single red rose between her hands, above her head.

The rose to me was an offering of love to the Creator.

Roses appear in accounts from all of the world's major religions as a symbol of miraculous love at work in the world. In ancient mythology, roses symbolized eternal love in stories of how gods interacted with each other and human beings. Pagans use roses as decorations to represent their hearts.

The fragrance of a rose represents the sacredness of people's souls.

Resilient Heart Art

Healing Heart Art #6

Painted: 8-10-2017

Title: Triple Heart Transformation Re-visited

I wanted to use the Triple Heart Transformation for the cover of my book, Resilient Heart: a holistic guide to a healthy heart for women, but the original was too fierce. That image was for me. In this image she is softer, yet powerful enough to survive 3 heart attacks. You can see the path of the heart beat going across the bottom of the image.

To signify the growth that has happened because of this heart journey a tree emerges from the top heart. It could represent a tree of life which is appropriate. The Tree of Life is more accurately described as the World Tree in the cultures of ancient Central and South American tribes.

These trees are depicted as having four branches extending in the four cardinal directions and roots that descend into water below. The roots are believed to be a representation of the underworld.

So, if we think of my heart as the earth plane the roots of the tree descend into it and reach up to connect my heart with heaven. This is where I connect and get powerful information. Also, the heart can be symbolized by water.

What a powerful image for rising from the depths of illness to reach up and touch the stars and be blessed.

Resilient Heart Art

Healing Heart Art #7

Painted: 8-21-2017

Title: Solar Eclipse

I painted this painting during a very powerful solar eclipse. Venus was in Taurus at 25 Degrees in the 6th house during the eclipse and Venus in my natal chart is in Taurus at 25 Degrees in the 5th house so that is what would be activated in me at the solar eclipse. Venus represents harmony and if we are attuned we naturally attract what will help us develop and be fulfilled. Venus is exalted in Taurus. The theme of harmony develops through the paintings.

In the painting there are nine hearts representing the phases of the eclipse, though in my journal I wrote "phases of the heart".

The message that came to me was " A new Love is coming onto the planet now. Higher, purer, more conscious. A radical change in the energy. It is a love portal and a heart opening time for everyone."

In the image the central heart is slightly higher and represents the inner child as creator who wants to play and create a new world. At the time of totality, I asked for another message. This is what I received: "You are witnessing a great shift on Planet Earth that will change the structures that have been in place for thousands of years. Priorities will change universally and in the USA.

Within your personal sphere of influence a shift is also occurring changing your inner structures and priorities. Cling to nothing for all is changing. It is crucial to release all structures of a negative nature that have caused challenge for you.

Resilient Heart Art

Healing Heart Art #8

Painted: 8-23-2017

Title: Heart Healing Mandala

This mandala was made specifically to assist in healing my heart. As you can see the main image is a six-pointed star, which is a symbol of the heart chakra, which is the energy center for the heart. In it's center is the Vesica Pisces which you will read about later in the book that was part of my dream. Bringing those images together into one image activates the power of the dream. Around the outside are various symbols.

The spiral represents movement. In the upper left corner and right middle are symbols for two of the archangels that I work with. Michael and Gabriel. Gabriel is the Archangel of healing.

The four spirals together are a Celtic symbol. When there are two or more spirals attached to each other, which most of the time describe a man's journey from his inner world to encompass the world beyond.

You see a symbol for healing in the lower left

Middle left is a powerful symbol for healing.

Green is also a healing color and purple brings the healing to a higher level. Healing mental, emotional and spiritual levels.

In the center of the Vesica Picses is the Eye of Horus. The eye of Horus is an ancient Egyptian symbol of protection, royal power and good health.

Resilient Heart Art

Healing Heart Art #9

Painted: 9-27-2017

Title: Metamorphosis

This image depicts the Heart as Chrysalis showing the stages of the three heart attacks and the stages of the heart if it is looked at through the lens of the chrysalis.

Heart Attacks are the Great Excavator if you allow them to work their magic. They will take you on a transformational and metamorphosis like no other. They will shake you to your core, strip you down, crack you open, throw you down, turn you into goo and send you back into the world like a new butterfly. It's a hell of a process! You will look like you don't know what you are doing. People will think you are unevolved because you have raw emotions. You will be judged and tossed aside, clearing the way for your real tribe to emerge. It will be raw and messy, you will wish you were dead, want to give up, try to run away. If you do you will miss your greatest opportunity. It takes deep courage and radical self-care to take the journey.

The butterfly captivates our hearts and imagination and has also become one of the most profound and enduring symbols of change and self-transformation. Its journey is one of pain and perseverance, struggle and triumph. The butterfly's journey and metamorphosis from humble earthbound caterpillar to winged beauty with the gift of flight, carries powerful meaning that speaks to our own capacity to move through different life cycles, mirroring our own journeys of regeneration, renewal, expansion and rebirth. That is what I wanted to depict in this image. We have a choice when we find ourselves in a life-threatening situation. We can think like a caterpillar or think like a butterfly. I am choosing to be the butterfly.

Resilient Heart Art

Healing Heart Art #10

Painted: 10-3-2017

Title: Butterfly Goddess

The Butterfly Goddess came out of the previous painting of the butterfly transformation in the chrysalis. She is empowered after being transformed. You will notice the Vesica Pisces, the six-pointed star, the lotus and a goddess rising from it, in her hands. She is a butterfly goddess, so she is about transformation. Butterflies are most often a symbol of the soul, so this Goddess is the protector of souls. She helps the human follow the soul's divine blue print.

There are several Goddesses who rose from lotus blossoms, the Hindu Goddess Tara being one of them. According to popular belief, she came into existence from a tear of Avalokiteshvara, which fell to the ground and formed a lake. Out of its waters rose up a lotus, which, on opening, revealed the goddess. Like Avalokiteshvara, she is a compassionate, deity who helps men "cross to the other shore." She is the protectress of navigation and earthly travel, as well as of spiritual travel along the path to enlightenment. She is perfect for the heart journey I have been on. There is actually a green version of Tara. She protects us from fear.

I placed the six-pointed star in the heart and the Vesica Pisces in the womb where they were in my original dream. The symbols place together like this enhance the Goddess' power centers.

Resilient Heart Art

Healing Heart Art #11
Painted: 10-19-2017
Title: Ancestral Bloodline

I was working on clearing bloodline issues, so this painting represents my ancestors and was taking tincture which is the flower in the painting.

From my journal:

"You have ancestral karma that goes back generations and you carried it forward this life because you are the only one who can break the karma once and for all generations going forward. It has to do with money. There have been paupers, beggars and those who lost everything in the Great Depression. Your grandfather on your father's side carried it."

This guidance made me realize I might be able to clear the cause of the heart attacks the ancestral connection to Elevated Lipoprotein (a). The heart is releasing the issues as the ancestors gather around. The blood is being returned to them purified.

Bloodroot is great for family protection and family luck. Nudges out physical, emotional, mental and spiritual genetic patterns inherited from generations of family members to make way for the light of new potential, so we can live as fully functioning humans. Use Bloodroot Flower Essence to facilitate transformation of genetic tendencies such as alcoholism, blood sugar imbalances, autoimmune disorders, depression, brain chemistry imbalances and heart problems. Bloodroot will assist your journey to full health. I had no idea that it was good for clearing blood sugar issues and heart problems! Those are my family issues.

Resilient Heart Art

Healing Heart Art #12

Painted: 10-27-2017

Title: Rose Elixir

From my journal: "I painted this and cried all day. Grief for the past nineteen months, for not having my life, for being sick all of the time, for meds that cause anxiety, for being used as a medical guinea pig, for not being heard or listened to, for losing three friends in the process, for going through this alone and having three back to back heart attacks. I want my life back!

So, I painted the heart of the tree and how the tree is being fed by roses that we don't even see. They are underground sending rose elixir through the roots of the tree. Roses represent miraculous love at work in the world. Miraculous love is feeding the tree, unconditionally. I have always thought of roses as a symbol for the heart.

Rose vibrates at the highest frequency on the planet, so it is uplifting. Reading the passage above I sure needed uplifting at that point and here is my soul sending me an image that would do that. The rose is much more than an ornamental flower adored for its heady aroma. The healing medicine of the rose is extraordinary and under-appreciated and using roses as food and medicine can offer us deep physical, emotional, and spiritual healing.

Rose medicine can be a wonderful way to soothe our aching hearts or lift us from deep grief. Rose elixir is exceptionally uplifting and can be used to relieve trauma, grief, depression, anxiety, heartbreak and chronic stress and fatigue. Here I am at a time of grief painting about rose elixir! This is truly a representation of the healing power of art.

Resilient Heart Art

Healing Heart Art #13

Painted: 11-3-2017

Title: Tree of Life and Heart of the Earth

I loved trees and have been attracted to the idea of The Tree of Life for a long time. It speaks to the earth/sky connection and have been a big part of my healing. When I painted this, I was having a lot of pain in my chest and was anxious about my heart. When I was anxious the trees would calm me down, especially the tree I adopted and named Grace. Staying calm was a moment by moment practice. I went into my studio and this is what came out.

The painting is full of beauty, new beginnings (the eggs), Life (the tree of Life) and change (the number 5) fertility (the earth) and it says that I am going to be amazing after the surgery. Life is actually coming out of the arteries in the form of eggs. The DNA is transforming into the tree of life. The crystalline core of the earth is sending energy to the heart. WOW! I usually don't get messages this fast, sometimes it takes years for me to understand what a painting is saying. This might not have meaning to anyone else, but it is profoundly healing to me.

I painted this November 3rd, 2 days before I learned I would have bypass surgery. I was picking up on something profound that would happen. If you look at the right side of the heart it looks like there is a bypass coming out of the side. It actually goes up and connects into the DNA/Tree of Life. I found out on the 8th that I needed to have the bypass, so 4 days after I painted this. base of the DNA in the painting that goes into the heart is almost the same as the actual bypass. The doctor drew the same pattern on the heart pillow to show my daughter what he had done. So, the painting tells me that the bypass has opened me to a new level of life.

Resilient Heart Art

Healing Heart Art #14
Painted: 12-7-2017
Title: Cosmic Womb

This was the first painting I did after open heart surgery. It took me four times longer because I couldn't see very well! This was two weeks after open heart surgery.

The morning I painted it I had had a dream. I don't remember much of it but this: We are all geniuses. Only a few people go through this kind of initiation. There is a special name for it that I don't remember. These kinds of initiations produce magic. I needed to put my heart in the protective womb of the Mother and let go of concern. Because it is visionary I don't always know right away what it is saying. This is what I learned afterwards.

This was inspired by the idea that the heart is the first organ to form in the early stages of the fetus. So, this heart is in the womb with an umbilical cord connected to the cosmic womb of the Divine Feminine. I feel that the heart continues to have a direct connection with the Divine and receives information all of the time from Source if we listen and pay attention.

The gold planet is the planet Venus, which is the planet of love. She also stands for reciprocity. Venus is a two-way street, being the planet of give and take. It has to do with generosity of spirit, which opens up the love and friendship flow. She is associated with self-expression, which then opens up the admiration flow. She supports you in cultivating your gifts, and that then affects your cash flow.

What is interesting about this is that ever since heart surgery I knew I needed to open and create a career with my art. It was time to dive in and just do it.

Resilient Heart Art

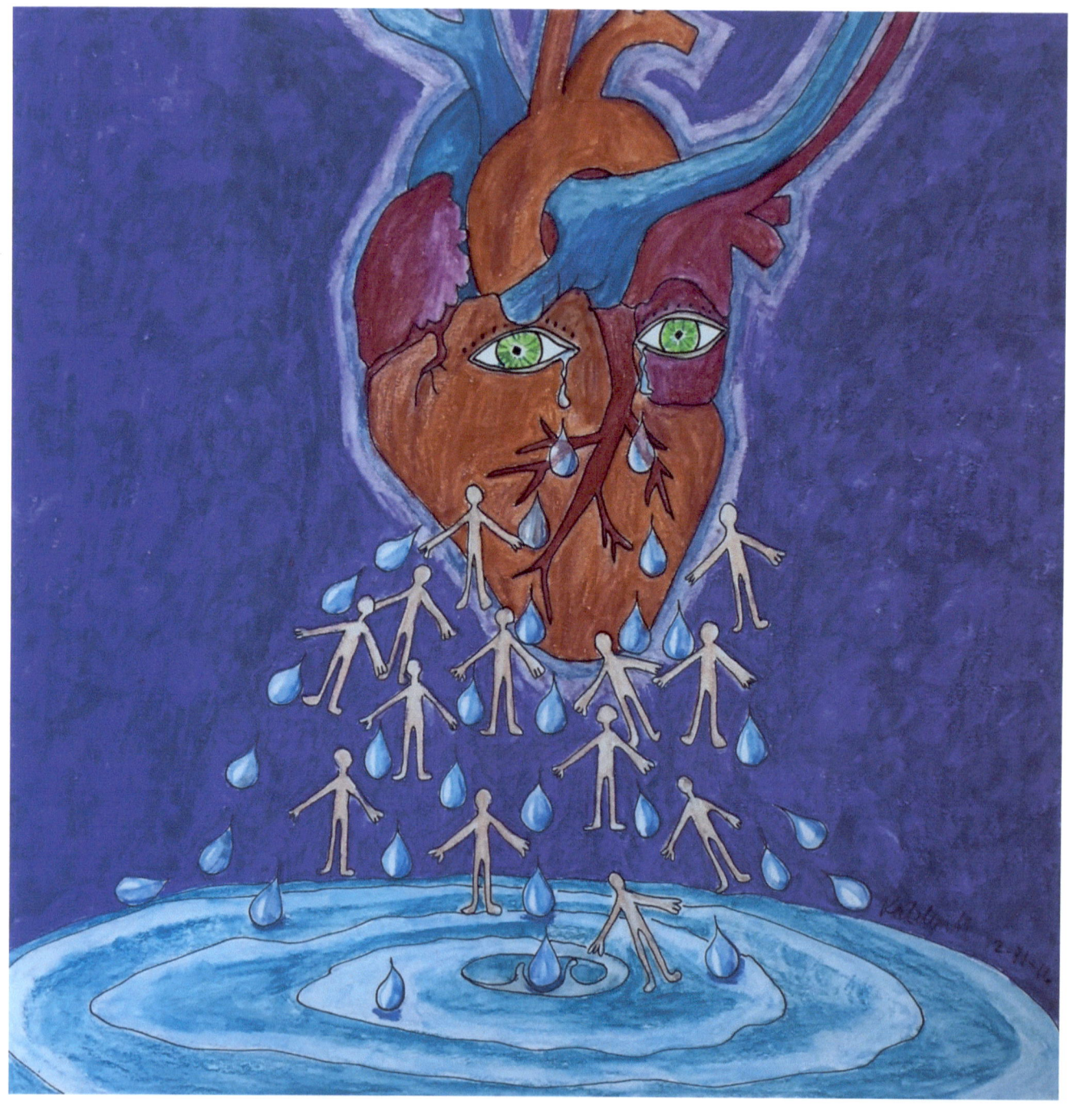

Healing Heart Art #15

Painted: 12-31-2017

Title: Tears of the Heart

I had a ton of energy the day I painted this when I hadn't had any before. I painted non-stop because two images wanted to be expressed, one after the other. A couple days earlier I watched a video of Kyle Cease, and a question he asked got a hold of me and wouldn't let go. The question "What is trying to emerge from me that I have never experienced before? What is my butterfly?" I asked it repeatedly. 2018 I was going to be my year of JOY, so that was mixed in with the question. I felt I couldn't experience joy because something was still in the way.

Out of the question the first image emerged in a sketch with a lot of tears. I felt sadness for my heart for what it had been through, not just physically but emotionally. There was a deep sense of sorrow both recent, past and ancient and universal and it could finally be released because my heart was now open, and I could feel it. I brought all of this into the first painting.

From my journal:

With every heart break my heart closed a bit more until it couldn't close any more at which point it had to attack itself 3 times. Finally needing to be opened surgically.

Sadness broke loose. Some named and some unnamed flowing now. Will it ever stop? I want to release it, I don't want to hurt any more. Will I ever experience happiness again? Love? Joy? I want to open to love and joy. Let it go. That is what I painted.

Resilient Heart Art

Healing Heart Art: 16

Painted: 12-31-2017

Title: My Hearts Butterflies

This image was painted right after image 15. I cried until there were no more tears and then this image came through.

From my journal:

I set my heart free of all of this sadness, grief and loss, so that I can emerge the butterfly. With a heart full of sadness there is not room for love and joy, the butterfly cannot emerge. The question "What is trying to emerge from me that I have never experienced before? What is my butterfly?" I kept asking it to myself over and over. The question got a hold on me and wouldn't let go! Near the end of the first painting the second image emerged. As I finished the first image I could see the second one in my mind's eye. Releasing the old energy allowed for a bridge to open up to the new energy. The bridge between one image and the other was profound. There was a minute second between on image releasing the old energy and the new image emerging to allow the new energy to come in. I had released the sorrow and it made room for "My butterfly" to reveal itself. Not just one butterfly, but 5 butterflies!

This is the transformational power of art at its finest. I followed my soul promptings, I got out of the way and it lead me where I needed to go. I am open now to let joy into my life and receive it. This was New Year's Eve and I set the intention to live in joy in 2018. Now I am open to the JOY that awaits me.

Resilient Heart Art

Healing Heart Art :17

Painted: 1-2-2018

Title: Engaging the Muse

Following the question as it answers itself is always magical. I find myself asking questions and letting them answer. This image roses from a question.

I was at a New Year's Eve party and we were talking about how to remember dreams. The idea came up about engaging the dream muse, so he knew you were serious about remembering. Would your attention and engagement be enough that she would help you remember your dream?

As I was falling asleep that night I pondered "What if you engaged the muses of your dreams and desires in the same way so they knew you were serious? Would they manifest because you were engaged? This took me to "What if you engaged the muse of your life that way? Not just giving it lip service, with fancy resolutions and big intentions. Truly engaging it as though it were a living energy. Taking it by the hand and running with it, rather than trying to be someone, do something or make something happen like we're taught. Would life feel your authentic engagement and lead you on an amazing adventure?

I know from experience that if you are not attached to outcome, living fully in the present, truly engaged with life unexpected magic will happen. What do you feel?

This painting, which wasn't planned out based on symbolic meaning, color placement, or anything preplanned. It sprang from my inner being in answer to this question "What would happen if you truly engaged with the muse of your life?" The muse being that creative force within that is your source of inspiration, your non-attached inner dreamer who creates magic. The genius that is in all of us.

Resilient Heart Art

Healing Heart Art #18

Painted: 2-25-2018

Title: Goddess with Cardinal

Symbolism: Cardinal

This Goddess is an alchemist. She is making something beautiful out of something that is not so beautiful, which is what I am doing with my heart concerns. As I was painting this cardinal popped onto her shoulder and began whispering in her ear.

I was curious to find out the metaphysical meaning of the cardinal. Here is what I discovered.

If Cardinal has flown across your path;

She is asking you to be clearer about your intentions. Setting a clear and insightful goal for yourself will accomplish everything you desire and more. Cardinal may be signaling you to be wary of what you are creating with your thoughts. Make sure that you are aware of exactly what you are manifesting and then make any corrections that are necessary.

This was perfect because I want to create a new life that is about doing what brings me joy and the voice of doubt sneaks in once in a while. Cardinal is telling you how to listen to your inner voice and intuition. You are in touch with your feminine side and capable of great sensitivity. Cardinal people tend to be initiators and are always the pioneer. The energy coming from Cardinal is that of a seer and a spiritual messenger. The crest on the head of the Cardinal brings the symbolic meaning of spiritual connection, importance and intelligence.

What a perfect messenger to have on your shoulder, whispering in your ear!

Resilient Heart Art

Healing Heart Art: #19
Painted: 3-23-2018
Title: Alchemy

I have always been intrigued by alchemy for personal transformation and this painting speaks to that. There are three stages of alchemy happening here. She starts out as a stone statue, from out of the statue she rises from beneath out of the mud and her transformed self-rises from there.

Spiritual alchemy is a grand experiment that you perform on yourself with deep introspection and objective investigation. Through the process you can regenerate yourself. This process often comes during some kind of crisis.

I feel my heart journey was a vehicle to transform myself. It became the worst thing that ever happened to me and the best thing that ever happened at the same time.

Spiritual alchemy is freeing yourself from your core wounds, core beliefs, any soul loss and other self-destructive structures. Through the process you can live freely without obstacles blocking your progress.

Paracelsus described alchemy as "The voluntary action of many in harmony with the involuntary action of nature. The center of the creative process place in the heart of man." I find that profound in light of my heart healing process.

The hope is to attain a state known as the Philosophers' Stone or Diamond Body. The process of achieving that is the spiritual rebirth through the union of opposites, the Sacred Marriage. The whole art of alchemy is contained within the image of the Magical or Divine Child. So, we continue to see the themes of the Sacred Marriage and the emergence of the Divine Child who for me is a part of me I left behind when I was four years old that I am rediscovering.

Resilient Heart Art

Healing Heart Art #20

Painted: 3-27-2018

Title: Solar Return Mandala

For my birthday I create a mandala to represent the energies that I intuitively feel coming in the solar year ahead. This is a Solar Return Mandala. From meditation: " This will be a seed to implant the energy of your connection to Goddess/God which will help it expand. Incorporate within the image the energies of Grace, Ease, Happiness, Health, loving relationship, Wealth, support, spiritual communication and flow. This will help you envision and create those things in your life.

I decided to use ancient runes for the energies and picked what is called Bind Runes from Iceland. These runes combine the energy of more than one rune.

In the center of the Vesica Pisces/Six-pointed star, which is the point of creation is a seed. In the center of the seed is a Yod, which represents the single point at which creation emerges. Unity and the Divine Spark with multiplicity.

Through my heart journey I have come to believe it is the combination of the Vesica Pisces and the six-pointed star and the point in the middle that creates a powerful vehicle for manifestation. There are reasons for each color.

The Runes:

Top left is the symbol for lasting partnership, top Right the symbol for Personal wealth and financial security, lower Left the symbol for Grace, Lower Right the symbol for health. The waves of energy on the outside of the six-pointed star give it energy and vibration so those things can manifest.

Resilient Heart Art

Healing Heart Art: #21

Painted: 3-31-2018

Title: Ensoulment

To me ensoulment is the process where the body and soul become one. It isn't the same as the soul coming into the body at birth but a metaphysical process that happens when you transform. This is when the heart and soul become one and you started living from your heart. At that point your heart is navigating, and your mind is just providing you with information, not directing the show. Of course, the soul does enter the child in the womb and that is the beginning of the ensoulment process, but I believe it isn't complete until we can live in unity between the heart and soul.

When I painted this, I was thinking about the impact of having 4 heart events on my heart. Each butterfly represents the transformation I went through to survive the event. You will notice the butterflies start out faded, which is my diseased heart. With each incident the butterfly gains more color until the last one shows a healthy butterfly merging with a healthy heart. The transformation is complete, and I am living with my soul united with my heart.

I chose this image for the cover for both of my books because it feels like completion of the transformation process. It is a hopeful image and speaks to higher levels of the psyche. Whoever looks at it will get something different all in a positive vein.

Resilient Heart Art

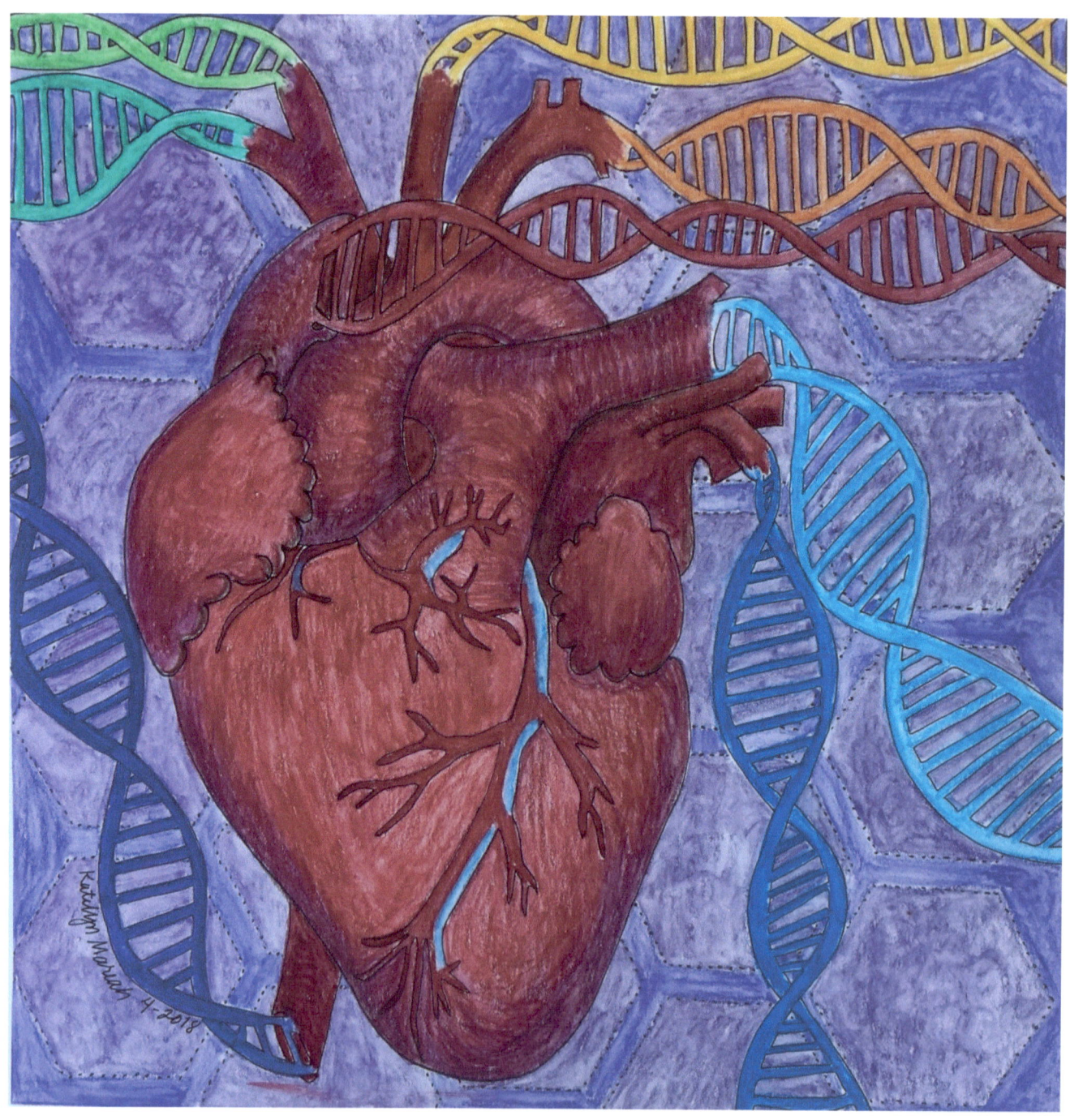

Healing Heart Art: #22

Painted: 4-1-2018

Title: The Light of DNA

This image is about a healthy heart having DNA of light flowing through it. It is strong DNA that keeps the heart healthy because the DNA has been reprogrammed to support heart health. Deoxyribonucleic acid (DNA) is a nucleic acid that contains the genetic instructions for the development and function of living things. The main role of DNA is the long-term storage of information. It is often compared to a blueprint, since it contains the instructions to construct other components of the cell, such as proteins and RNA molecules. The DNA segments that carry genetic information are called genes. Other DNA sequences have structural purposes or are involved in regulating the expression of genetic information.

Some believe that the DNA is on autopilot and you can disrupt that and reprogram it to be healthy and free of disease. The science of Epigenetics supports this idea. I was thinking about that process in this painting. The DNA is painted in rainbow colors and is flowing into the arteries.

My heart attacks were caused by and inherited issue Elevated Lp(a). I believe it might be on both sides of the family. It causes early strokes and early heart attacks and 63 Million people carry this gene. My thought with this image was that I could go into my DNA and shut off the gene that expresses as Elevated Lp(a). Some might think this is fantasy, but the mind and intention are powerful things.

Resilient Heart Art

Healing Heart Art: #23

Painted: 4-3-2018

Title: Small Strands of DNA

This is the violet flame an energy that helps us transmute negative thoughts. The violet flame can heal emotional and physical problems, improve your relationships, help you to grow spiritually, or just make life easier.

You can see the strands of DNA dropping into the violet flame surrounding the heart. Those are negative thoughts and beliefs that can lead to disease. The violet flame changes vibration at the atomic level, changing negative energy into positive. By transforming negative thoughts and feelings, the violet flame provides a platform for our healing.

The violet flame is an invisible spiritual energy, the seventh ray, that appears violet to those who have developed spiritual vision. It's the highest frequency in the visible spectrum. To the ancients, this transcendental color was a spiritual rather than a physical phenomenon. It has the power to erase, or transmute the cause, effect, the memory of our past mistakes. Transmutation means to change - to alter in form, appearance or nature. The violet flame changes negative energy into positive energy, darkness into light, "fate" into opportunity. On the physical level, the violet flame can help heal our bodies by removing issues that make us vulnerable to illness and disease. The real cause of disease is often rooted in our mental, emotional and spiritual states.

I believe anything is possible with focused attention, trust and letting go. That is why I am still here after 3 heart attacks and open-heart surgery.

Resilient Heart Art

Healing Heart Art #24

Painted: 4-6-2018

Title: The Compass of the Heart/North star

I felt like I was in an indescribable, incredible, new space where there was no pressure to do anything to make something happen when I painted this. I believed that the things I desire are just going to happen, which was new for me. I am not worried about anything even though there are worrisome things in my life at the time.

I asked in meditation what this space was. "You are feeling what it means to live in your heart, your center and in balance. There is no fear or worry in that space no matter what is going on in your outer world because you know it is all for your highest and best/Soul purpose. This is the space from which miracles and magic occurs." That is True North and the Compass of the heart.

"You don't have to do anything for this alignment has already occurred and you can't stop it from happening. Alignment happened the day of the heart attack when you had the dream of The Sacred Marriage. The six-pointed star from the ceremony is the compass that was placed in your heart that is pointing to your True North that is where your partner is. This doesn't necessarily mean he is in the north. The compass of your heart is activated by your inner marriage/Sacred Marriage, where you came into balance with the male and female in you. The Sacred Marriage occurred and activated the magnetics of your heart compass." I sat and looked at this and remembered that I had gotten this information before. I remembered at the time I was really intrigued by the idea and purchased a compass necklace. I painted the compass in my heart to represent My True North.

Resilient Heart Art

Healing Heart Art #25

Painted: 4-19-2018

Title: Guadalupe, the Heart of Compassion

After I paint a painting I usually do some research because I don't know the meaning behind an image, I am just following my inspiration. My images come from other dimensions/ realms.

There was a lot of amazing symbolism that I discovered about this painting. There is a symbol embroidered in the red dress of Guadalupe that stands for The Heart of the Universe. It is in the same exact place where I painted the heart/my heart which suggests a direction connection to the heart of the Universe and my heart. The gold symbolism on her dress in the original image over her womb is "The Heart of the universe" The heart of the universe lies in the womb of her body and I intuitively painted an actual heart there!

The shape of her aura, which is known as the mandorla, is always depicted as the center of the Vesica Pisces which signifies the marriage of the sun and moon. The Vesica Pisces possesses healing powers, immense power and energy. It can rid one of worry, anxiety and panic according to my research. Right before I painted this I had made a commitment to release those things.

My painting is the completion of the sacred marriage in my heart. If I think about this painting on a deeper level, the Vesica Pisces was placed in my womb, in my dream, to assist me in birthing a new self. Here is Guadalupe holding my heart. She has stepped out of the center of the Vesica Pisces/Mandorla, holding my transformed heart, filling it with her essence before giving it back to me.

Resilient Heart Art

Healing Heart Art #26
Painted: 4-24-2018
Title: Intercessory Angel

Intercessory Angel of Heart Health, whose name is Cassiopeia.

There is an interesting shift that happened here that I didn't notice Right away. I had been calling the paintings heart healing paintings and it switch to heart health.

Looking up information on Cassiopeia was interesting. It means "she whose words excel". Cassiopeia is a constellation, "the enthroned and beautiful", that has the five stars named after the five brainwave states: Epsilon, Delta, Gamma, Beta and Alpha. I have been studying them the last couple of weeks. I had no idea of this connection.

I found a novel with a story about Cassiopeia, called The Winds of Wexford. Here is an interesting description of Cassiopeia:

"By means of her innate grace, exquisite beauty and magical lyricism, Cassiopeia is the ultimate paradigm of the Principle of Divinity and the chosen one who shares her love with a great angelic warrior, known as a hero among the angels of heaven. Her mission upon Earth is to set in motion a sequence of events intended to awaken the deep unconscious of sleeping human being to unleash the energies of the Great Unfolding of Human Evolution. For Cassiopeia the power of transformation exists in the love she feels for her other half. Only he knows who she is.

I have always believed that my art and writing is intended to help people awakening and transform so the New World can unfold. I have always felt that I had a partner and together we would work toward that purpose. Having connected with this Angel through this painting means a lot to me and is very affirming.

She is holding my healthy heart which radiates love to all the world.

Resilient Heart Art

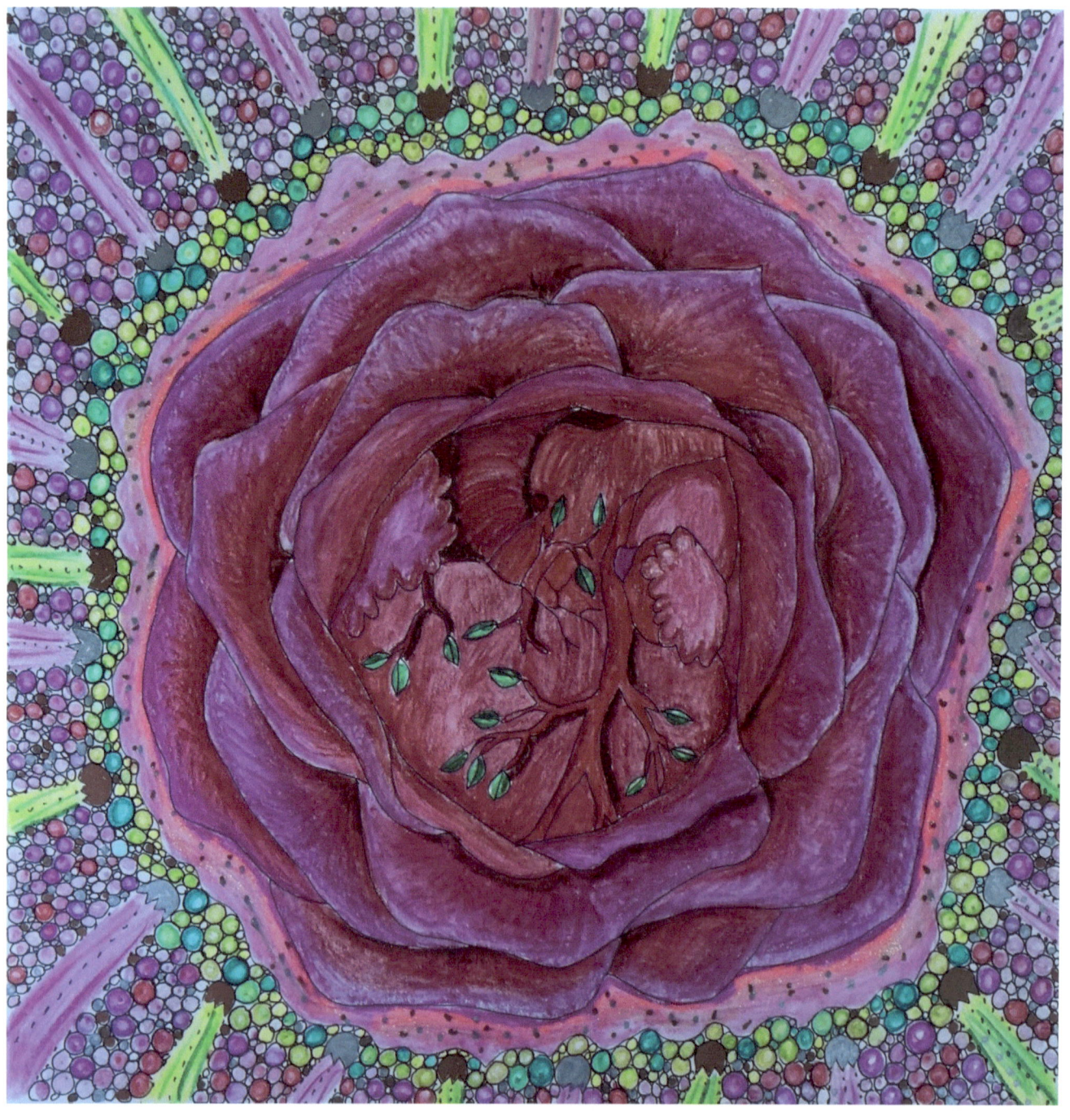

Healing Heart Art #27

Painted: 4-29-2018

Title: Rose of the Heart-The Mystic Rose

One of the most beautiful and significant symbols of the Western Mysteries is the Rose. The Rose and the Holy Grail share many spiritual resonances. The word 'chalice' comes from the Latin word, calyx, which means cup, and is the name given to the cup-like sepals of a flower which support the petals. Both suggest the receptive vessel of the soul, opening to receive the in-pouring of Divine influence.

The symbolism of the Rose is even more complex than the Grail, given its beauty, the number and arrangement of the velvety textured petals, the intoxicating perfume and the hidden golden heart enfolded deep within the petals, concealing the Mystery of the Centre. Inside of the rose in this painting resides the healthy, opened heart. The heart is an organ of great mystery.

In medieval Europe, the Rose symbolizes union with the divine which influenced Arabian and Persian teachings. The Sufi teacher, Hazrat Inayat Khan writes:

"Just as the rose consists of many petals held together, so the person who attains to the unfoldment of the soul begins to show many different qualities, (which is what happened to me). The qualities emit fragrance in the form of a spiritual personality. (My personality has changed in so many ways.) The rose has a beautiful structure, and the personality which proves the unfoldment of the soul has also a fine structure, in manner, in dealing with others, in speech, in action. The atmosphere of a spiritual being pervades the air like the perfume of a rose."

Resilient Heart Art

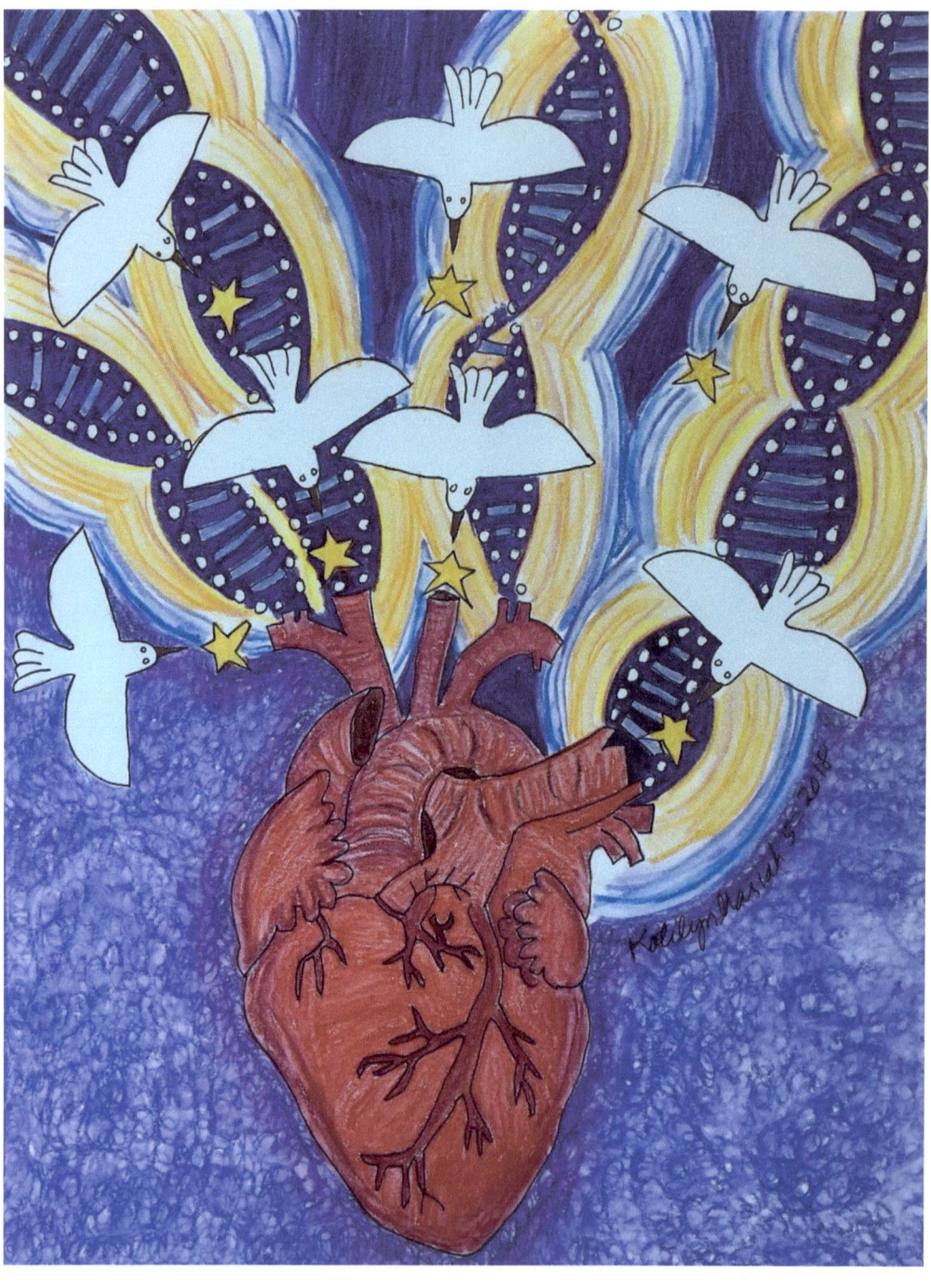

Healing Heart Art #28

Painted: 5-1-2018

Title: 7 Doves of the Heart

I just listen and paint. This was the painted message today. When I researched what it might mean this is what I found!!

Seven doves are symbols of the Pleiades constellation, that is represented by seven stars. The Pleiadean's are of a fifth dimensional frequency, which is one of love and creativity. The Pleiadeans share higher consciousness through the DNA. This consciousness is radiating outwards like a beacon, creating shafts of golden light streaming, that are free flowing, that are interacting with your own multidimensional energy allowing a rebirthing process within your awareness. These light streams interact and anchor within your heart cells. This prepares the heart to open to love.

The Pleiadeans are believed to be highly evolved. The Pleiadean Realm is the next step or level in our human evolution. It is for this reason that certain knowledge is being given to us by specially enlightened Pleiadean beings. There are those that want to help us toward our higher spiritual destiny. They bring us the frequency of higher love consciousness.

Doves teach us that, regardless of external circumstances, peace is always a touch a way, within us, and always available. It is said that if a dove flies into your life, you are being asked to go within and release your emotional disharmony. The dove helps us to rid the trauma stored deep within our cellular memory. Doves carry the energy of promise. Releasing disharmony was the thing I was working on because I knew it would help my heart heal even more deeply.

The dove's roles as spirit messenger, maternal symbol and liaison impart an inner peace that helps us to go about our lives calmly and with purpose.

Resilient Heart Art

Healing Heart Art #29

Painted: 5-2-2018

Title: Double Swan

Swan's Wisdom includes awakening the power of self, balance, inner beauty, innocence, self-esteem, understanding dream symbols, seeing into the future, understanding spiritual, evolution, developing intuitive abilities, divination, grace in dealing with others and commitment. It is associated with love, poetry and music. The swan was sacred to Venus, the love goddess in Roman mythology. In Celtic tradition the Swan represents the Soul, our eternal essence.

The Swan teaches us that we all have inner grace and beauty, and this teaches us self-esteem. As we begin to realize our own true beauty, we reveal the ability to bridge new realms and new powers. Swans graceful entering into your life signals a time of altered states of awareness and the development of intuitive abilities, for those with this medicine have the inherent ability to see the future, and to accept the healing and change that is starting in their lives. Accept this and it will help you go with the flow. Listen to your inner knowledge and intuitions and Swan will work through you.

This image represents partnership as well. I am finally open to having a conscious partnership with a man, which my broken heart would not allow. Swans form a classic image of devotion, with their curved necks entwined in a perfect love heart. This is part of the courtship ritual, in which the pair faces each other and with a ruffle of feathers and lifting of wings, they bow gracefully. Once courtship is complete, the male and female swan are bonded for life. They are said to learn from each other as they raise young year after year and improve their successes by learning from their failures.

Resilient Heart Art

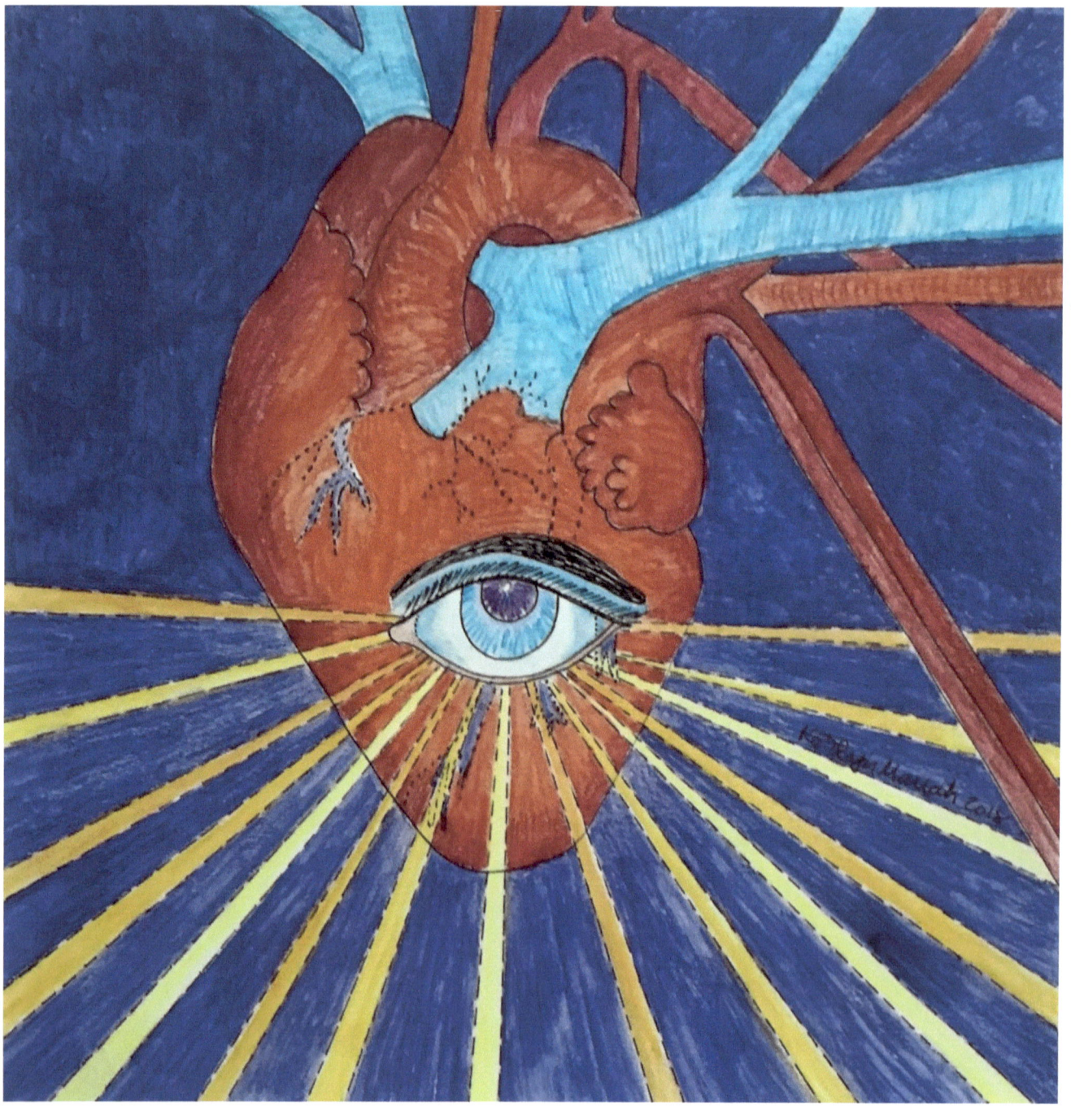

Healing Heart Art #30

Painted: 5-6-2018

Title: The Eye of the Heart/Chante Ishta

This is my painted interpretation of Chante Ishta.

I was listening to Gregg Braden on YouTube talk about Chante Ishta which is a Cherokee word meaning the single eye of the heart. This is Heart wisdom that does not judge anything as good or bad, it is just neutral. It is in the moment and all is as it should be. The heart speaks a spiritual language that doesn't always translate into words. Sometimes there aren't words for what we see, feel, experience and only an image can express it. The beauty of a painting is that you don't need to understand it because it is speaking to your soul and trying to find words takes something way from your experience.

The world's most powerful language is a mixing of thought, feeling and emotion which is the language of Chante-Ishta. This powerful language that has no words, the language of the heart, can move mountains. The key is learning to experience feelings and experiences without judgment, bless the experience for bringing insight and accept and resolve pain. Using the eye of the heart that does not judge we can turn our experiences into beauty and the healing of the body comes naturally.

I had spent a year exploring my resistance in its subtle manifestations and had come to a place of free flow and movement because I wasn't judging what was happening to me but seeing it as the most transformational gift that it was.

We are asked to bless the things that cause us pain out loud. The verbal expression opens your heart and releases the charge of judgment and replaces it with beauty in everything.

Resilient Heart Art

Healing Heart Art #31

Painted: 5-7-2018

Title: Infusing and Emerging Consciousness

This is Ganesh the remover of obstacles. I have developed a strong relationship with him after an encounter with him in Bali in 2014. He has become a confidant during this heart transformation. This image is about reciprocity, the giving and receiving of compassion.

This is a standing Ganesh dancing on the heart and rising out of the lotus of the heart. He is infusing Ganeshness, which is Ganesh intelligence, into the heart It is infusing and emerging at the same time.

Visualizing your heart as a lotus flower can create safe, comfortable space for your mind to settle. In Eastern scriptures, the inner awareness, the Inner Heart, is depicted as a lotus flower. If our consciousness can be visualized, then it would be through the lotus flower.

Once again, the metaphor is perfect for the healing process for the lotus springs out of the mud and slime and reaches its way up to blossom into a beautiful flower. The healing process is the same thing. What was the worst experience of my life, became the most transformational experience of my life at the same time because I allowed it to move away from the mud and slime that created the heart attacks to transform me into a thing of beauty.

I allowed Ganesh to dance with me as I healed my heart and he helped me remove any obstacles in the way of my healing.

Resilient Heart Art

Healing Heart Art #32

Painted: May 17-2018

Title: Completion

This image brings together symbolism that has followed me through this journey into a completed mandala. I wasn't thinking about creating a mandala, I was following the image as it came to me. I later realized it was a mandala that spoke to the integration of all my healing work the last two years.

According the Carl Jung the Mandala is a graphical representation of the center of the Self. It can appear in dreams and visions or it can be spontaneously created as a work of art. Usually the mandala is a geometrical form, such as a square or a circle and can be abstract and static, or a vivid image formed of objects and/or beings.

Jung refers to the mandala as "The psychological expression of totality of the self." Within everyone's psyche, there is a seed center of the self which is surrounded by a chaotic maelstrom of issues, fears, passions and countless other psychological elements. It is this disorder that creates emotional imbalances that contribute to disease. The mandala is a template for the mind used to create a state of peace and order, so that resolution of the chaos can reorganize into a whole.

It indicates the phenomenon of centering of the ego in relation with the psychic wholeness. It is part of the individuation process described by Jung in his works. In the Jungian therapy, which includes the recognition and the conscious integration of the contents of the collective unconscious, the spontaneous drawing of mandalas is required.

It is not without importance for us to appreciate the high value set upon the mandala, for it accords very well with the paramount significance of individual mandala symbols which are characterized by the same qualities of a - so to speak - "metaphysical" nature. Unless everything deceives us, they signify nothing less than a specific center of the personality not to be identified with the ego. Carl Jung

In this image we have the symbols I have followed through the process, the heart, the butterfly, the Vesica Pisces, the six-pointed star and the lotus. But you will notice a new symbol appears as well: The egg and the nest. They are symbols of new life and new beginnings. The nest is the foundation that will hold the egg while it develops. I feel that it speaks to the new life I am creating from transforming myself. I can't go back to where I was but am invited to re-invent my life.

This is what I know right now. I also know that my images will continue to speak to me for years to come, revealing new information as I am open to receive it. If you use this book and the images as a meditation the same will happen with you. My comments are only suggestions of possible meaning.

I also encourage you to start an art practice to work on your current issue or something that seems to be blocked in your life. It doesn't have to be elaborate art. Remember the process is more important than the final product. I have been painting since I was a child and watercolor has been my medium for 25 years, so it is easy for me to paint visionary images. By no means should you stop yourself because you judge your art. Everything you create has great value.

CHAPTER SIX
ABOUT KATELYN MARIAH

What you should know about me.

I have been an artist since I was a child when I painted my first purple, three-legged cow. No one could tell me there was something wrong with it because it came straight from my imagination. I was hooked! I wanted to be an artist when I grew up!

I built my first studio, all by myself in my parent's basement when I was a teenager. I built the walls, the drawing table and the easel. I just made them up without plans to follow. This room became my sanctuary.

Art is in my blood and in my soul. I follow my muse and when I get information I paint it. I love painting.

I have formal training in art and art therapy with a BFA from studies at The Minneapolis College of Art and Design and the University of Minnesota, which uses oil paint and egg tempera. I have classical training in a rare Renaissance painting technique called the Mischtechnik. Yet my real art doesn't come out of formal training. I taught myself how to connect to something higher, how to listen and how to paint what I am seeing in my vision.

I became a visionary artist in the early 1990's

What the heck is visionary art, you might ask? Fair question.
For some it happens when using psychedelic drugs. Some come by it naturally without the use of drugs. I am the latter.

My understanding of Visionary Art as it came into my life.

In 1991 my third eye spontaneously opened up and a blue ray shot out of my forehead. My boyfriend of six years saw it and was shocked. I didn't realize what had happened because I wasn't in my waking up process at that point. That sure put me on that path very quickly!!! We broke up soon after that, his idea. I imagine it scared him and he didn't know how to process it.

Soon after that I began having visionary art experiences. As you read, I didn't realize what I was tapping into at first.

I believe my third eye and pineal gland were activated. The pineal gland and third eye are the eye of mystical awareness. The pineal gland secretes the chemical DMT (Di-Methyl-tryptamine), which creates lucid visioning and induces mystical experiences. I became a mystic and frankly that scared me.

My art is visionary because of the process of lucid visioning. Images just drop into my third eye that contain, ancient wisdom, wisdom from the future and transformational information, that comes from a higher consciousness. I usually don't understand what it means until I do research, but I listen, trust what comes to me and I paint it. You can look at one of my paintings and maybe not understand what you are looking at, but you are touched at a soul level.

I might be somewhere and can't capture the images in paint, which happens in my car a lot. Yet the image stays with me until I can paint it. That is how the 44 images for Awakening the Goddess happened. That was my first major visionary project.

"The pineal gland has long been thought to be the seat of consciousness and tied to both mystical practices and psychedelic effects of DMT." Dr. Rich Strassman conducted serious experiments on DMT and the pineal gland in the 80's and 90's and thought this to be true as well. Cultures around the world have suggested a connection between the third eye and pineal gland.

Rene Descartes coined the Pineal gland as "the seat of the soul" because he believed it provided people with a medium from which our soul could be expressed through our physicality.

Word, symbol and image are so interesting to me, because they can have so many different meanings to people. Symbol, color, movement, and shape are the language of the soul. I am intrigued by the deeper subtler meanings of things and how you can look at an image and it speaks those subtle meanings to the soul where it is understood on a deep level.

This is my psychic gift and what I am here to do. Even though I have painted 100's of paintings I have put my gift on hold several times for a number of reasons. Often it was because I couldn't support myself financially and paint, a common theme with artists. Maybe another reason was that people might go away like my boyfriend did because they don't understand. That happened a lot too. That's okay with me now. I can't not paint any longer. It was detrimental to my heart!

Now that my heart is open and healed I am in a prophetic, prolific state right now and images are coming one after another like they did when my Goddess Deck was created, that is why I am painting so much. My higher consciousness has something to say. These are the images in this book.

View more of my artwork at www.katelynmariahvisionaryartist.com

Katelyn Mariah BFA, MA, LICSW

www.katelynmariahvisionaryartist.com

www.mystickcreekpublishing.com

www.empoweredhealthandwellness.com

Mystickcreekpublishing@gmail.com

651-955-3673

Resilient Heart Art